GREAT SPORTING EVENTS

Football

Clive Gifford

W
FRANKLIN WATTS
LONDON • SYDNEY

Franklin Watts

First published in Great Britain in 2016 by The Watts Publishing Group

Copyright © The Watts Publishing Group, 2016

Editors: Katie Dicker & Gerard Cheshire
Art Direction: Rahul Dhiman (Q2AMedia)
Designer: Rohit Juneja, Cheena Yadav (Q2AMedia)
Picture researcher: Nivisha Sinha (Q2AMedia)

Picture credits:
t=top b=bottom c=centre l=left r=right

Front Cover: Laurence Griffiths/Getty Images
Back Cover: NZPA, Ross Setford/AP Photo, Aijaz Rahi/AP Photo, Dave Thompson/AP Photo, Mark J. Terrill/AP Photo, Jay LaPrete/AP Photo, Anja Niedringhaus/AP Photo.
Title page: Thomas Kienzle/AP Photo.
Imprint Page: Mel Evans/AP Photo.
Insides: Paul White/AP Photo: 4, Celso Pulpo/Shutterstock: 5, Manu Fernandez/AP Photo: 6, Jeff J Mitchell/Getty Images: 7, Clive Brunskill/Getty Images: 8, Paul Hilham/Getty Images: 1 & 9, Topical Press Agency/Hulton Archive/Getty Images: 10, Lewis Whyld/AP Photo: 11, Yves Logghe/AP Photo: 12, Cosmin Iftode/Dreamstime: 13, Themba Hadebe/AP Photo: 14, Rebecca Blackwell/AP Photo: 15, Fernando Llano/AP Photo: 16, Photo Works/Shutterstock: 2 & 17, Katonia82/Shutterstock: 18, Matthias Schrader/AP Photo: 19, Luca Bruno/AP Photo: 20, Robert Cianflone-FIFA/FIFA via Getty Images: 21, Dmitry Lovetsky/AP Photo: 22t, Thomas Kienzle/AP Photo: 22b, Katonia82/Shutterstock: 23, AP Photo: 24, AGIF/Shutterstock: 25, Ng Han Guan/AP Photo: 26, Leszek Wrona/Dreamstime: 27, AP Photo: 28.

ISBN: 978 1 4451 4964 6

Note: At the time of going to press, the statistics in this book were up to date. However, due to the nature of sport, it is possible that some of these may now be out of date.

Printed in China

Franklin Watts
An imprint of
Hachette Children's Group
Part of The Watts Publishing Group
Carmelite House
50 Victoria Embankment
London EC4Y 0DZ

An Hachette UK Company
www.hachette.co.uk

www.franklinwatts.co.uk

FSC MIX Paper from responsible sources FSC® C104740
www.fsc.org

Contents

Words in bold are in the glossary on page 30.

A game of goals

Football, also known as soccer, is a game of goals. Two teams compete for the football, move it around the **pitch** and try to kick or head the ball into their **opponent**'s goal. It is the world's most popular team sport, with hundreds of millions of fans who watch games and play the sport themselves.

Barcelona's former goalkeeper Victor Valdes makes a fingertip save in a match against Spanish rivals, Real Madrid.

Men and women

Football is played by teams of 11 players. Whilst casual games may be mixed, separate competitions for men's and women's football exist. These include the USA-based professional competition for women, NWSL (National Women's Soccer **League**). This new league began play in 2013 and has attracted some of the world's best female footballers.

Club football

Nearly all football is played in leagues (or **divisions**) which feature a number of football clubs. The clubs usually play each other twice in a **season,** although in some smaller leagues, teams may play each other more frequently. Most leagues award a club three points for winning a match and one point for a draw.

Promotion and relegation

At the end of a season, the bottom team or teams in most leagues are **relegated**. This means they start the next season in the league or division below. Teams from this lower division take their place by being **promoted**. Some leagues, such as the Major League Soccer (MLS) in the United States and Canada, have just one division, so there is no promotion and relegation.

International football

Footballers play for clubs in different countries, but the very best get the chance to play for their own country's national team in international matches. Some internationals are friendlies – games played for no overall competition or prize. Others are crucial qualifying games in which teams have to do well to get the chance to play at major tournaments such as the **FIFA** World Cup (see pages 22–27).

GREAT SPORTING STATS

The World Cup is the biggest football prize of all and Brazilian footballer, Pelé, is the only player to have won it three times (1958, 1962 and 1970). Considered one of the greatest players of all time, Pelé scored 77 goals for Brazil and over 1,280 goals during his career. These included more than 90 hat-tricks (three goals in a game).

Cristian Gamboa of Costa Rica and Luke Shaw of England compete for the ball during a 2014 FIFA World Cup match.

The big leagues

The wealthiest football clubs are mostly found in Europe. They play in the continent's biggest leagues, such as Serie A in Italy, Spain's La Liga or the English Premier League (see pages 8–9).

Serie A

Italy's Serie A grew from 18 to 20 clubs at the start of the 2004 season. It has traditionally been one of the richest leagues of all, with its clubs making the first £1 million, £10 million and £30 million signings for top players. Juventus, with 31 championships, is Serie A's most successful side.

La Liga

The top league in Spain is home to many of the world's most famous footballers, including Cristiano Ronaldo (Real Madrid) and Lionel Messi (Barcelona). Teams play 38 games over the season and the bottom three teams at the end of the season are relegated from La Liga. Only three teams have never been relegated: Athletic Bilbao and the two most dominant sides, Real Madrid and Barcelona, who have won La Liga 55 times between them.

Rafa Lopez of Getafe attempts to tackle Barcelona's Lionel Messi during a pulsating game in La Liga.

The Bundesliga

The German Bundesliga began in 1963 with 16 teams (now expanded to 18). Each team plays each other at their home ground and away at their opponent's ground. At the end of the 34-game season, the bottom two teams are relegated to the league below, whilst the third bottom team plays the third top team of the lower division. The winner starts in the Bundesliga the following season.

Scottish Premiership

This 12-team league (the top division of the Scottish Professional Football League) has an unusual format. All the teams play each other three times in a season. The league is then split into top and bottom halves with the teams playing the other five in their half for a fourth time.

GREAT SPORTING STATS

The French Ligue 1 has been won by 19 different teams since it started in 1932. However, Olympique Lyonnais (Lyon) won seven championships in a row from 2002 before Bordeaux finally broke their run in 2009.

Lee McCulloch rises to head the ball goalwards for Rangers in a SPL match against their fierce rivals, Celtic. The two teams have won the Scottish league more than 90 times between them.

The English Premier League

The English Football League was established in 1888 and featured four divisions. In 1992, the teams in its top division, First Division, broke away to form the Premier League. It is now one of the most-watched and supported leagues in the world.

Home and away

In 1994, the number of teams in the Premier League was cut from 22 to 20. Each of these teams plays one another, home and away, during the season, which starts in August and ends in early May. Played in famous **stadia**, packed with passionate fans, matches are often fast, furious and exciting. Millions of people tune in to watch live games or highlights on television.

Money matters

Sponsorship by companies and the sale of tickets, souvenirs and television **rights** have made the Premier League one of the wealthiest in the world. It was estimated that the money coming in to the 20 clubs in the 2014/15 season totalled £1,605 million.

Liverpool fans cheer their team on during an English Premier League match against Chelsea.

Ryan Giggs is the only player to have won 13 Premier League championships. On his retirement in 2014, Giggs had appeared in 22 Premier League seasons (and scored in 21 of those seasons). His 632 Premier League appearances were all for the same club, Manchester United.

Top and bottom

Manchester United have won an impressive 13 Premier League titles. At the other end of the table, a massive battle takes place to avoid finishing in the bottom three places and being relegated to the Championship. Some 46 teams have played in the league since its introduction in 1992. Only half of the 22 who played in the Premier League's 1992/93 season were in the league for the 2014/15 season.

Foreign imports

In 1992, there were just 11 footballers in the Premier League who were not from Britain or Ireland. The Premier League's increasing wealth has allowed clubs to employ some of the best foreign footballers around, from France's Eric Cantona in the past to Yaya Touré from the Ivory Coast and Spain's Francesc Fàbregas in more recent times. In 2013/14, there were 373 foreign players in the Premier League. Just five English players took part in all of their club's 38 matches.

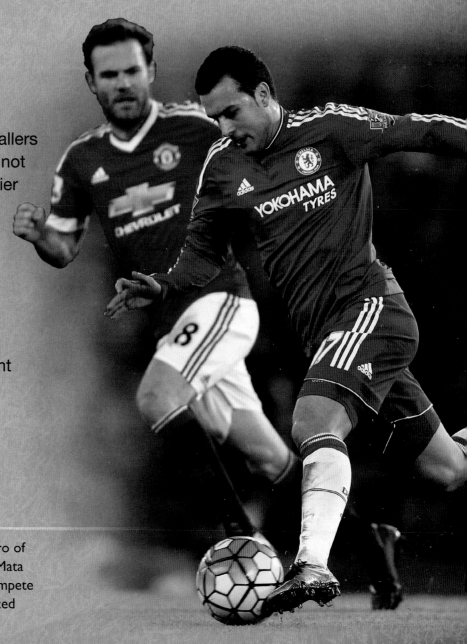

Two Spanish players – Pedro of Chelsea (in blue) and Juan Mata of Manchester United – compete on the ball during a fast-paced Premier League match.

The FA Cup

The FA Cup, which began in 1871, is the oldest major cup competition in the world. Today, it features over 730 English and some Welsh clubs, but the tournament attracts interest from around the world. The 2014 Cup final between Arsenal and Hull City had an estimated television audience of 500 million people.

Early start

The FA Cup competition begins every August when **amateur** teams take part in the 'Extra Preliminary Round'. The teams that enter the competition at this point have 13 matches ahead to reach the final. In January, the Third Round is held, when teams from England's top two divisions enter the competition. The FA Cup final is held at the end of the Premier League season in May.

Bolton Wanderers play West Ham United in the 1923 FA Cup Final, the first held at the newly-completed Wembley Stadium in north London. Bolton won the game 2-0.

It's a knockout

The FA Cup is a **knockout** competition, with the number of teams halving after each round of matches. There are no **seeds** and opponents are picked at random. There is only one match unless the game is a draw, in which case there is a replay at the other team's ground. If that game ends in a draw, **extra time** is played. If the game stays drawn, it is decided with a **penalty shootout**.

Giant killers

One of the great appeals of the FA Cup is that smaller teams get the chance to play the top teams. If they win, they are labelled 'giant killers'. Famous giant-killing acts include Liverpool losing to Bristol City in 1994, Barnsley knocking both Chelsea and Liverpool out of the competition in 2008, and Bradford City beating Chelsea in 2015.

GREAT SPORTING STATS

The most successful teams in the FA Cup have been Arsenal (12 wins), followed by Manchester United (11 wins), and Tottenham Hotspur (8 wins). Aston Villa and Liverpool follow with 7 wins each.

Temporary home

The FA Cup final was held at Wembley Stadium, London, from 1923 until 2000 when the stadium was rebuilt and the final moved to the Millennium Stadium in Cardiff, Wales. The final returned to the new Wembley Stadium in 2007.

An aerial view of Wembley Stadium in north London. It holds 90,000 spectators.

The UEFA Champions League

A cup competition for the winners of Europe's different national leagues began in the 1955/56 season and was won by Spain's Real Madrid. The European Cup became the **UEFA Champions League** in 1992. It has grown into the biggest and richest cup competition for football clubs in the world.

One of the 32

Clubs who finish top or second of the biggest leagues in Europe are guaranteed one of the Champions League's 32 places the next season. Other teams who win smaller leagues or who finish third or fourth go into a series of preliminary games starting in July. The Champions League competition itself begins in September.

Group games

The 32 teams are seeded and divided into eight groups of four teams who play each other at home and away. They get three points for a win and one for a draw. The top two teams in each group progress to the last 16 stage. From here to the final, it is a knockout competition with pairs of teams playing each other (home and away) and the winner going through to the next round. The final is a single match held in a different European city each year. In 2015, it was held at the Olympiastadion in Berlin, Germany.

Dutch midfielder Clarence Seedorf was the first footballer to win the UEFA Champions League with three different clubs.

Intense interest

Europe is where most of the world's greatest and most famous footballers play club football, so there is worldwide interest in the Champions League. This has been helped by great moments such as England's Wayne Rooney scoring a hat-trick for Manchester United on his Champions League **debut** aged just 18, or Liverpool's astonishing comeback from 3-0 down to win the 2005 Champions League Final against AC Milan.

A money game

The sale of television rights, as well as sponsorship and advertising, has made the Champions League the wealthiest football competition of all. More than €1 billion (£770 million) was paid out to the 32 teams who took part in the 2014/15 tournament. The winners, Barcelona, received over €60 million (£46 million).

Spain's Real Madrid, with ten European Cup or Champions League wins and three runners-up places, is the most successful team in the Champions League. It is followed by Italy's AC Milan (7 wins), England's Liverpool (5), Germany's Bayern Munich (5) and Spain's Barcelona (5). No one has yet played more Champions League games than Italy's Paolo Maldini who has appeared in 139 matches.

The Barcelona team celebrate with the Champions League trophy after beating Italian giants Juventus in the 2015 final.

The African Cup of Nations

In 1957, three national football teams, Egypt, Sudan and Ethiopia, met in Sudan to play in the very first African Cup of Nations. Organised by the Confederation of African Football, the tournament is now held every two years.

Egypt's Ahmed Fathi tackles Samuel Inkoom of Ghana during the final of the 2010 African Cup of Nations.

In season

The tournament is held over two or three weeks in January. This is the middle of the season for the European football leagues, where many top African footballers, such as Kolo Touré of the Ivory Coast and Cameroon's Alexandre Song, play. This sometimes leads to clashes with European clubs not releasing players for warm-up games. Since 2013, the tournament has been moved to odd-numbered years, to avoid a clash with the World Cup.

Tournament format

As African football has boomed, the number of teams entering the tournament has increased. Since 1998, the tournament has admitted 16 teams from the 50 or so African nations who enter the qualifying competition. These 16 teams are then split into four groups of four who play each other.

Tense finish

Whilst some tournament games have seen clear wins, the final match in the competition has often been close and tense. Eight finals have needed a penalty shootout for a winner to be determined, the latest in 2015. In 1992, it took 24 penalty attempts before the Ivory Coast managed to beat Ghana 11–10.

Winners

Teams from all over Africa have won the tournament, from Morocco in the north in 1976, to South Africa 20 years later. Egypt won the very first tournament and has won a further six since, including the 2010 competition, making them the most successful team. They are followed by Ghana and Cameroon, each with four championships.

GREAT SPORTING STATS

African Cup of Nations
- **Most tournament goals:**
  18 – Samuel Eto'o (Cameroon)
- **Most tournament appearances:**
  8 – Ahmed Hassan (Egypt 1996–2010) and Rigobert Song (Cameroon 1996–2010)
- **Most goals in a single tournament:**
  9 – Mulamba Ndaye (Zaire, 1974)

Cameroon fans cheer after hearing their national anthem at the start of an African Cup of Nations group match.

The Copa America and the Gold Cup

South America, along with North and Central America, have their own continental competitions for national teams. Both the Copa America and the Gold Cup have long histories. In recent years, the Gold Cup has been held every two years and the Copa America every four.

The Copa America

The Copa America first took place in 1916. Argentina, Uruguay and Brazil usually dominate the competition. The ten national men's football teams that form the South American Confederation (CONMEBOL) take part, along with two teams chosen from other FIFA confederations, to make 12 teams in total. From 1997–2007, Brazil won four out of five tournaments. Chile was a surprise first-time winner in 2015.

Brazil's players rush forward as their teammate Gilberto Silva scores the winning penalty that sees them beat Uruguay and reach the final of the 2007 Copa America.

GREAT SPORTING STATS

Guillermo Stábile is famous for being the first player to score a hat-trick at a World Cup in 1930. But he is also the Copa America's most successful coach, winning six competitions with Argentina between 1941 and 1957. During his reign, Argentina notched up the Copa's biggest win by beating Ecuador 12–0.

Carlos Pena of Mexico (in green) and Gabriel Torres of Panama in action during the 2013 CONCACAF Gold Cup.

The Gold Cup

CONCACAF is the organisation that runs football in North America, Central America and the Caribbean. Their regional competition, the Gold Cup, has been through many changes, and since 2000 has included 12 teams from these countries. The Gold Cup is usually **hosted** by the United States or Mexico but in 2015, Canada hosted a few games, too. The United States and Mexico met in the final in 2011 at the Rose Bowl stadium, California, where over 93,000 people watched Mexico win.

Guest teams

Both competitions have invited teams from outside of their region to take part to increase competition, fan interest and revenue. South Africa in 2005, South Korea in 2000 and 2002, and Brazil and Colombia on three separate occasions, have taken part in the Gold Cup. Mexico and Jamaica were guest teams at the 2015 Copa America, and will take part again in 2016, joining the United States.

The European Championship

The European Championship, or 'Euros', is a tournament for the leading national teams of Europe. It began in 1960 and has gone through many changes in format, but is now established as a major international competition.

Hosts and teams

Different countries bid to host the European Championship and three times (in 2000, 2008 and 2012), two neighbouring countries have shared the task. The first European Championship, won by the Soviet Union, featured just four teams. This was expanded to eight in 1980 and then 16 in Euro 96, held in England. Host countries automatically gain a place in the tournament.

Robin van Persie of the Netherlands (in orange) fights for a ball with Holger Badstuber of Germany during their 2012 UEFA European Championship tie.

Euro shocks

Over the years, there have been some major shocks in the European Championship. England failed to qualify for Euro 2008, whilst Greece, a team not thought of as a likely winner, won Euro 2004. Back in 1992, Yugoslavia pulled out of the competition and Denmark was invited to play at the last minute. Many of their players were on holiday, but they turned up and won the tournament!

UEFA European Women's Championship

The European Women's Championship began in 1991 and has been held eight times. Norway won in 1993, but otherwise, Germany has been utterly dominant, winning the seven other championships. The latest competition was held in 2013 in Sweden where Germany beat Norway 1–0 in the final.

Germany's Inka Grings (centre) was the top scorer at the UEFA European Women's Championship in 2009, with six goals – a tournament record.

Recent European Men's Championships

Year	Hosts	Winners Runners-up
2012	Poland/Ukraine	Spain 4–0 Italy
2008	Austria/ Switzerland	Spain 1–0 Germany
2004	Portugal	Greece 1–0 Portugal
2000	Belgium/ Holland	France 2–1 Italy
1996	England	Germany 2–1 Czech Republic
1992	Sweden	Denmark 2–0 Germany
1988	West Germany	Netherlands 2–0 USSR
1984	France	France 2–0 Spain

Olympic football

Football has been at the Olympics for over a hundred years. It was the sport's leading international competition before the World Cup. In recent years, the Olympics has attracted strong football teams from all over the world.

Young players

Only amateur footballers were allowed to play in the early Olympics, but in more recent years, all players can be **professionals**, providing 15 out of the 18-man **squads** are under the age of 23. Recent Olympic tournaments have seen world stars such as Lionel Messi and Sergio Agüero (Argentina) and Cristiano Ronaldo (Portugal) play, whilst Ryan Giggs captained the GB team at the London 2012 Olympics.

Olympic venues

Whilst most Olympic sports are held in and around the host city, football has often made use of a country's major stadia. The 2012 Olympics were based in London, but games were played at stadia around Great Britain including Manchester United's Old Trafford stadium, the Millennium Stadium in Cardiff, Wales, and St James' Park, Newcastle, with the final played at the new Wembley Stadium in London.

Argentina's Nicolas Pareja (right) climbs above Nigeria's Peter Odemwingie to win a header during the men's football final at the Beijing 2008 Olympics.

Getting to the games

Over 180 nations attempt to qualify for the 16 places at the Olympics men's tournament. One is given to the host nation, whilst competition is intense for all other teams. The men's teams of Argentina, France and Germany, for example, all failed to qualify for the 2012 Olympics. The GB team (England, Scotland, Wales and Northern Ireland) took part as the host nation in the 2012 Olympics but did not qualify for the 2016 Rio Olympics.

Women's Olympic football

Women's football finally reached the Olympics in 1996 in a tournament won by the USA. Women's teams have no age restriction, so top female players such as Brazil's Marta Vieira and the USA's Abby Wambach have been able to compete for a highly-prized gold medal. The USA team has so far been the dominant side, with four gold medals out of five. Germany holds the record for the most Olympic goals in a women's game, with an 8–0 defeat of China at the 2004 Olympics.

GREAT SPORTING STATS

Men's Olympic gold and silver medallists

Year	Gold	Silver
2012	Mexico	Brazil
2008	Argentina	Nigeria
2004	Argentina	Paraguay
2000	Cameroon	Spain
1996	Nigeria	Argentina
1992	Spain	Poland

Women's Olympic gold and silver medallists

Year	Gold	Silver
2012	USA	Japan
2008	USA	Brazil
2004	USA	Brazil
2000	Norway	USA

The USA women's team celebrate scoring against Japan at the 2012 Olympic Games in London.

The World Cup

The FIFA World Cup was first held in 1930 in Uruguay, South America. It has since grown into an enormous competition, the biggest single sport event in the world. Over a billion people watched the 2014 final between Germany and Argentina on television.

World Cup hosts

The World Cup finals are held once every four years. Countries bid many years in advance for the right to host the competition, which can attract several million visitors and much world attention. Almost all tournaments have been hosted in Europe or North or South America. The 2002 tournament was the first to be held in Asia and the first to be hosted by two countries, South Korea and Japan. The 2010 competition was the first to be staged in Africa and the 2018 tournament will see Russia host the event for the first time.

The original World Cup trophy was given to Brazil for good in 1970 after they won the World Cup for a third time. The new World Cup trophy (above) was designed by sculptor Silvio Gazzaniga.

Germany's Thomas Linke (left) challenges Brazil's Ronaldinho during the final of the 2002 World Cup, the first held in Asia.

France (in blue) and the Ukraine battle for the ball during a vital qualifying match for the 2014 FIFA World Cup.

GREAT SPORTING STATS

Each world region is awarded a number of places at the World Cup finals. Here were the places offered for the 2014 tournament:
- Europe: 13
- Africa: 5
- South America: 5 (plus the hosts, Brazil)
- Asia: 4
- Oceania: 0
- North America, Central America and the Caribbean: 4 places.

The last four regions each provide a team that takes part in play-offs for the final two World Cup places.

Qualifying campaigns

Thirteen teams attended the first World Cup finals. The tournament expanded to include 24 teams in 1982 and then 32 in 1998. With over 200 nations wanting to attend, all teams except the hosts must take part in a series of regional qualifying matches. Different continents use different systems. South America, for example, places all ten teams in one league where they play 18 games in total against each other.

Team disappointment

Only Brazil has reached every World Cup finals tournament. Many famous footballing nations have failed to get through qualifying matches. For example, before reaching the final of two World Cups in a row (1974 and 1978), the Netherlands had failed to qualify for the previous six tournaments. England failed in 1994 and Russia missed out on the 2010 tournament.

The ultimate prize

All 32 World Cup teams and their supporters dream of winning the World Cup. More than 200 countries enter the qualifying stages, but only eight have ever won this special prize. As five-time winners, Brazil is the most successful team, followed by Italy with four World Cup victories.

World Cup format

Once all 32 teams have qualified, they are put into eight groups of four teams who play each other once. The top eight teams based on world rankings are seeded. If the host nation is not among the top seeded teams, it takes one of these slots and the eighth team loses its position. These teams cannot be drawn in the same group as each other. The top two teams qualify from each group into a round of 16, followed by a **quarter-final**, **semi-final** and the World Cup final.

Brazil's Pelé (left) shoots during the 1970 World Cup semi-final against Uruguay. Brazil beat Italy in the final to win their third World Cup.

Scoring feats

At the 2006 World Cup, Sweden's Marcus Allbäck scored the World Cup's two thousandth goal in a match against England. The biggest 2014 win saw Germany thrash Brazil 7–1, whilst the most goals in a tournament game was an astonishing quarter-final in 1954 which saw Austria beat Switzerland 7–5.

Tense matches

Whilst some games are clear victories, many are tense, tight and won by a single goal. These can be just as exciting to watch as high-scoring matches, such as Senegal's 2002 shock defeat of France (then existing World Cup holders). At the 2006 World Cup, two of the quarter-final games and the final needed extra time and then a penalty shootout to determine the winner.

Germany celebrate beating Argentina to win the 2014 FIFA World Cup final.

Awards

FIFA's technical committee decides on who will receive a number of awards at the end of a World Cup. The highest goal scorer of the tournament wins the Golden Boot award. The World Cup's best player is given the Golden Ball award, which in 2010 was won by Uruguay's Diego Forlán and in 2014 by Lionel Messi from Argentina.

GREAT SPORTING STATS

Leading World Cup finals goal scorers.

17	Miroslav Klose (Germany)
15	Ronaldo (Brazil)
14	Gerd Müller (Germany)
13	Just Fontaine (France)
12	Pelé (Brazil)
11	Klinsmann/Kocsis (Germany/Hungary)

The Women's World Cup

A World Cup competition for the best women's national sides kicked off in China in 1991 with 12 teams. It has since expanded to include up to 24 teams, with the finals held once every four years.

Qualifying matches

A total of 45 national teams played matches to try to qualify for the 1991 World Cup. This figure grew to 119 teams for the 2007 tournament. With competition increasing, the 2015 World Cup expanded the number of teams at the finals to 24.

Finals format

The 24 teams are divided into six groups of four. Each team in a group plays the others, with the best two teams from each group reaching the knockout stage, as well as the best four third-placed teams. From then on, extra time is played if the game is drawn. If extra time doesn't reveal a winner, the teams play a penalty shootout to decide who goes through to the next game or wins the final.

Norway's Ragnhild Gulbrandsen scores with a header against Canada in their 2007 FIFA World Cup match.

Attracting spectators

Early fears that women's international matches wouldn't attract large numbers of fans proved unfounded. A crowd of 65,000 at Tianhe Stadium in Guangzhou, China, watched the final in 1991, whilst the 1999 final at the Rose Bowl stadium, California, USA, saw a record attendance of 90,185 fans.

The 2015 Women's World Cup

Over 1.35 million fans attended the 2015 tournament's 52 games. England had their first victory over Germany (after 18 defeats and two draws) but the most dominant team was the USA. In the final, they beat Japan 5-2 (the highest-scoring final in the history of the Women's World Cup). They also beat Germany's record as the top scoring team with 112 goals. The USA's Carli Lloyd scored the first ever hat-trick in the tournament's final.

A giant screen shows the USA women's team holding aloft the 2015 Women's World Cup trophy.

GREAT SPORTING STATS

Top goal scorers of all time in Women's World Cup football are:
1. Marta (Brazil) 15
2. Birgit Prinz (Germany) 14
3. Abby Wambach (USA) 14
4. Michelle Akers (USA) 12

1848 The first football rules are drawn up at Cambridge University.

1862 The first football club in the United States is formed, the Oneida Football Club, in Boston.

1863 The Football Association is formed in England.

1871 The first FA Cup, the world's oldest surviving cup competition, is held.

1872 The first football international match between countries ends in a 0–0 draw between England and Scotland.

1872 Laws of football introduce corner kicks.

1878 Whistles are used by referees for the first time.

1891 Penalty kicks are introduced.

1901 South America's first international match is held – Uruguay v Argentina.

1904 FIFA is formed.

1908 The first Olympic Games to feature football as a medal sport is won by England.

1912 A new rule is introduced to stop goalkeepers handling the ball outside of their own penalty area.

1930 The first World Cup competition is held in Uruguay and won by Uruguay.

1950 The largest attendance at a football match (over 199,000 people) is recorded at the Maracanã Stadium for the World Cup final between Brazil and Uruguay.

1957 The first African Cup of Nations is held in Sudan and won by Egypt.

1960 The first European Championship is hosted by France.

1975 Italy's Giuseppe Savoldi becomes the first million pound footballer when he moves from Bologna to Napoli football club for £1.2 million.

1991 The first Women's World Cup is held in China.

1992 The European Cup competition is reformatted as the UEFA Champions League.

1994 The World Cup is held in the USA for the first time. It is the first World Cup final to be decided by a penalty shootout.

1996 Women's football is included at the Olympic Games for the first time.

2009 Women's Professional Soccer League competition begins in the USA.

2010 The World Cup is hosted in South Africa, the first to be held on that continent.

2015 The seventh Women's World Cup is held in Canada.

The great Brazilian player Pelé shoots during the 1970 World Cup.

Winner tables

FIFA World Cup winners

Year	Winners	Runners-up
2014	Germany	Argentina
2010	Spain	The Netherlands
2006	Italy	France
2002	Brazil	Germany
1998	France	Brazil
1994	Brazil	Italy
1990	West Germany	Argentina
1986	Argentina	West Germany
1982	Italy	West Germany
1978	Argentina	The Netherlands
1974	West Germany	The Netherlands
1970	Brazil	Italy
1966	England	West Germany
1962	Brazil	Czechoslovakia
1958	Brazil	Sweden
1954	West Germany	Hungary
1950**	Uruguay	Brazil
1938**	Italy	Hungary
1934	Italy	Czechoslovakia
1930	Uruguay	Argentina

** (1942 and 1946 – no tournaments due to World War II).

FIFA World Cup highest scorer winners

2014	James Rodríguez (6 goals)
2010	Thomas Müller, David Villa, Wesley Sneijder, Diego Forlán (5 goals)
2006	Miroslav Klose, Germany (5 goals)
2002	Ronaldo, Brazil (8 goals)
1998	Davor Suker, Croatia (6 goals)
1994	Hristo Stoichkov, Bulgaria and Oleg Salenko, Russia (6 goals)
1990	Salvatore Schillaci, Italy (6 goals)
1986	Gary Lineker, England (6 goals)
1982	Paolo Rossi, Italy (6 goals)
1978	Mario Kempes, Argentina (6 goals)
1974	Grzegorz Lato, Poland (7 goals)
1970	Gerd Müller, Germany (10 goals)
1966	Eusebio, Portugal (9 goals)
1962	Garrincha, Vavá, Valentin Ivanov, Florian Albert, Leonel Sánchez, Drazan Jerkovic (4 goals)
1958	Just Fontaine, France (13 goals)
1954	Sándor Kocsis, Hungary (11 goals)
1950	Marques Ademir, Brazil (8 goals)
1938	Leonidas da Silva, Brazil (7 goals)
1934	Oldrich Nejedly, Czechoslovakia (5 goals)
1930	Guillermo Stábile, Argentina (8 goals)

FIFA Women's World Cup

Year	Winners	Runners-up	Tournament top scorer
2015	USA	Japan	Célia Sasic, Germany (6 goals)
2011	Japan	USA	Homare Sawa, Japan (5 goals)
2007	Germany	Brazil	Marta, Brazil (7 goals)
2003	Germany	Sweden	Birgit Prinz, Germany (7 goals)
1999	USA	China	Sun Wen, China and Sissi, Brazil (7 goals)

Glossary and further info

Amateur Players or teams who are not paid to play football.

CONCACAF Short for the Confederación Norte-Centroamericana y del Caribe de Fútbol, the regional organisation that runs football in North and Central America.

Debut A player making his first appearance for a team, or a team making its first appearance in a particular competition.

Division One of the groups of teams which make up a league. Teams in each division are of a similar standard.

Extra time A way of deciding a match in the event of a draw. It involves two equal length periods of additional play.

FIFA Short for the Fédération Internationale de Football Association, the international governing body of football.

Host The country or city that holds a football tournament.

Knockout Competitions where the winner of a single match or pair of matches progresses to the next round and the losing team is out.

League A type of competition format, where a number of teams all play each other with points awarded for a win or draw and a team's standing shown in a league table.

Opponent The team or individual players from that team that your team play against in a match.

Penalty shootout A method of deciding a drawn game by a series of penalties all taken at one end of the pitch.

Pitch The playing area for a game of football.

Professional Player who is paid to play for a football team.

Promotion Moving up a division of a league in club football.

Quarter-final The four games played with the four winners taking part in the semi-final of a competition.

Relegation Dropping down to a lower division of a league in club football.

Rights The business deal or deals that allow a company to show football matches on television.

Season The period of the year in which football is played in a country.

Seeds Highly-rated teams which are not selected to play each other at an early stage of a competition.

Semi-final The two games played with the two winners taking part in the final of a competition.

Sponsorship Payment made to a professional football player or team by a company to help promote or advertise their goods or services.

Squad The group of players from whom a manager or coach selects the eleven that will start a match as a team.

Stadia Plural for the word stadium.

UEFA Short for Union of European Football Associations, the governing body of football in Europe.

Websites

http://www.fifa.com/en/index.html
The official website for the organisation that runs world football, FIFA's website is packed full of news and features on the men's and women's game as well as details of all the World Cups.

http://www.worldcup-history.com
Lots of facts and figures on previous World Cups are available here in a database searchable by player or team.

http://www.uefa.com
The homepage of the Union of European Football Associations, the organisation that runs the European Championship and the Champions League.

http://www.thefa.com
The official website of the English Football Association with news on the England national team, English clubs and league tables and the FA Cup.

http://www.worldstadiums.com
The definitive guide to sports stadia around the world with details of those used in Olympic, World Cup and European Championship football.

http://www.premierleague.com
The official website of the English Premier League contains details of fixtures, results and many features on teams and players.

http://www.bundesliga.de/en
The English language version of the official website of the top German league, the Bundesliga.

http://www.mlssoccer.com
The official website of Major League Soccer, the leading men's soccer competition in the United States.

http://nwslsoccer.com
The official website of the National Women's Soccer League, which began play in 2013.

http://www.concacaf.com
The official website of CONCACAF which governs football in North America and the Caribbean.

http://www.planetworldcup.com/LEGENDS/wcstars.html
A selection of profiles on many great footballers, including top World Cup players.

Further reading

The Kingfisher Encyclopedia of Football – Clive Gifford (Kingfisher 2010/2016)
An in-depth guide to football, its history and great players and competitions.

FIFA World Football Facts and Records – Keir Radnedge (Carlton Books, 2011)
A large volume containing all the leading football records and facts.

Wicked World Cup 2010 – Michael Coleman (Scholastic, 2010)
A book of fun facts about the World Cup.

Know Your Sport: Football – Clive Gifford (Franklin Watts, 2010)
Find out about key football skills, techniques and team tactics in this practical guide.

Index